Celebrating Life

Other "Spiritual Companions"

Working with Angels
Making Prayer Work
The Act of Meditation
The Way To Health
Healing Emotional Wounds
Defeating Evil and Sin
The Role Death Plays in Life
The Noble Mind & Its Uses
Finding Meaning in Life
The Connection

Celebrating Life

by Robert R. Leichtman, M.D. & Carl Japikse

ENTHEA PRESS
Atlanta, Georgia & Columbus, Ohio

CELEBRATING LIFE

Copyright © 1976 by Light

All Rights Reserved. No part of this book may be used or reproduced in any manner without written permission, except in the case of brief quotations embodied in articles and reviews. Printed in the United States of America. Direct inquiries to: Enthea Press, P. O. Box 251, Marble Hill, GA 30148.

ISBN 0-89804-806-0

Introduction

Celebrating Life was first published under the title *Joy* as part of a set of 30 essays written by Robert R. Leichtman, M.D. and Carl Japikse on **The Art of Living.** It can be found in Volume I of that series, also titled *Tapping Our Rich Potential.*

It has been selected to be reprinted in this special gift edition because of its practical value in helping people learn to celebrate life. In an age when many adults suffer from depression and live lives of "quiet desperation," this book offers a remarkable antidote.

For information about ordering other issues in the **Spiritual Companions** series—or **The Art of Living**—please see page 92.

Something Extra

8

𝒜 recurring theme in many old parables and scriptures is that the Lord of the Universe has spread a magnificent banquet for us all, a board laden with ambrosia and nectar of the highest quality. All of us are invited, but few actually do partake in the feast. That's because there are two halls in which the feast is being served. One is real and the other is counterfeit, but the illusory banquet is sufficiently impressive that the vast majority of people mistake it for the real one. They are quite content with it, even though the food is neither nourishing nor satisfying. It does not occur to them that they have settled upon their lowest expectations, and have thus deprived themselves, by not thinking, of the real feast. They are dimly aware that they have been promised a certain something extra in life, but they believe that they have found it—notwithstanding the fact that they still hunger and thirst, even in the midst of seeming plenty.

In the art of human living, there are many qualities that give a wholly new dimension to life when we learn to express them: peace, harmony, love, beauty, and wisdom, to name a few. But there is one which deserves special consideration, for it is an essence which can justifiably be called the ambrosia and nectar of mankind. It is a certain "something extra" unknown to the average man or woman, but nonetheless a quality which will transform the life of the individual who learns to express it. It lifts life out of the realm of the humdrum, the ordinary, and the uncreative into the sphere of the harmonious, the purposeful, and the productive. It adds a new sparkle, a new enthusiasm, and a touch of good humor. It helps us become more mature and capable of expressing confidence in the purposes of life, even when the tides of events may seemingly be flowing in opposing directions. It is the quality of *joy*.

Undiscerning people trapped in the hall of the illusory banquet have no real understanding of what joy is. They believe that the "something extra" of life can be found in the conventional state of good feelings. They talk profoundly about "bliss" and smile wanly, convinced that they have found something worthwhile—as they sup and sip from nothingness.

Joy cannot be known in the hall of illusion, for it exists only in the banquet of reality. It can, however, be cultivated by those who wish to do so. Indeed, the cultivation of joy is well worthwhile, for joy is indispensable to the art of living. It is a celebration of intelligent involvement in the universe: of creativity, of healing, of participating with the One Life. But it must be properly understood if it is to be developed. For joy is an intangible quality which exists independently of mankind in the universe, although it can be contacted by men and women and blended into their lives. It has a reality of its own; it is not the invention of mankind, nor is it the conjuration of man's imagination.

This notion may be upsetting to those who believe that they can create their own universes in their imaginations—who think that whatever they happen to believe in is right for them. This is an interesting theory, but hardly one that matches reality. Such people generally assume that joy is just the same thing as happiness or feeling good. They lead bland, lukewarm lives—uninspired, unfulfilling, and lacking in any real achievement. But they desperately want to believe that they have accomplished something of importance in their pursuit of mediocrity, so they talk loudly about their great feelings of bliss and peace, hoping someone will believe them and help sustain their somewhat fragile illusion.

It is an error to blur the distinctions between joy and the emotional states of happiness and feeling good. It is just such careless thinking which leads us into the hall of the counterfeit banquet in the first place. And once we find ourself there, there is only one way we can find the way out: through more careful and precise thinking. We can begin by comparing the three states of happiness, feeling good, and joy.

Happiness is a state of emotional contentment. Most people would define it as the absence of hardships and problems, and therein lie the roots of illusion. Happiness has no real substance—it is most often just a neutral state in which the emotional waters are calm for a period of time. Of course, happiness is sometimes produced by participation in activities one likes, but such instances are only of secondary importance. After all, if a person is disturbed by some problem in his life and racked with worry and fear, then the mere involvement in a hobby or activity which he traditionally likes will not lead to happiness. So, for most people, the state of happiness is essentially the state of "not being unhappy." And it is a fragile state, for it is not based upon the fundamental realities of the universe, but rather upon the evanescent likes and dislikes of the individual's personality. Happiness tends to be sentimental in character, heavily colored by selfish interests and personal prejudices, lacking any real depth or foundation. Made of superficialities, it crumbles under the touch of the person who grabs for it and tries to hold on to it. It is never permanent; the first problem that arises will shatter it.

Feeling good is an illusion of the same magnitude. Feeling good can be defined as the quest for pleasant emotional sensations, which are sought in a variety of ways: through the "ultimate" experience of sex, the "ultimate" empathy of watching a soap opera, the "ultimate" high of taking drugs, and so on. In each instance, the individual is seeking an outside stimulus which will make a strong impact upon his or her emotions and produce an artificial sensation. Such sensations literally induce a massive commotion in the individual's emotional body (as seen clairvoyantly)—a commotion that most closely resembles utter chaos but which nonetheless seems to appeal greatly to many people. The state of feeling good can, of course, create a feeling of happiness for the short duration of the sensation—a happiness which may indeed linger for awhile after the sensation ceases. But eventually the repeated quest for the pleasure of feeling good will lead to emotional exhaustion, intense unhappiness, and depression.

Both happiness and feeling good are emotional states—states of being focused on the astral or emotional plane. They are emotional responses to outside events and stimuli and are thus entirely dependent upon the nature of one's experiences at any point in time. If all is going as hoped, then happiness and good feelings result; if not, then frustration, despair, or grief are sure to ensue. In either case, the need for happiness and good feelings becomes an addiction, and the individual's center of consciousness becomes focused almost exclusively on the emotional level. While the unimaginative would undoubtedly disagree, it is nonetheless an occult truism that the emotional plane is the very heart of the banquet of illusion. The individual who pursues happiness and good feelings becomes entrapped in that illusion, believing them to be the "something extra" he has sought. As a result, his life remains incomplete.

Manifestly, the quest for happiness and good feelings is not enough to fulfill the purpose of our humanity. After all, a certain kind of happiness is sometimes achieved by people in most repulsive ways. It is known that Adolph Hitler was quite happy after the Nazi victory over France. Similarly, malicious gossips seek their emotional highs in the titillation of dragging the good names of other people through mud and slime. It would be hard to argue with any conviction that such states of happiness and feeling good lift up the human spirit or contribute to the advancement of mankind.

In contrast, the genuine "something extra" is a quality which is greater than both happiness and feeling good. It is a state of being which does not find its impetus in emotional sensations or any external events. It does not fade during periods of unpleasant circumstances and hardship; it does not wither in the face of opposition or bitterness. It does not prey on the misfortunes of others, nor spring from the wells of selfishness or personal prejudice. Rather, it is an abiding presence which is entered into only when one begins sharing in Universal Consciousness. It is not the expression of a need (as is happiness), but rather an expression of fulfillment.

While happiness and feeling good are emotional reactions to the events which happen to us, the bonafide "something extra" is a creative energy which molds, shapes, and above all else *acts*. It pushes outward from within, as an impelling force which permeates the whole being of an individual. It is not an indifferent state of not having anything amiss; it is a dynamic, affirmative state of knowing that there is meaning and order in the universe, that we are sharing in that universe, and that this is right and proper, fundamentally good. In short, it is a celebration of the reality of life, both individual and universal.

Such, then, is **joy**. It is neither an emotion nor a feeling, but rather a universal quality which links us with all other universal expressions of life—when we express it. It has its origins and existence in the realm of the mind, in the banquet of reality. It is part of the landscape of the mental plane, and as such is a reflection of the bliss of the atmic plane (to use occult terminology). Joy, therefore, is a mental energy, an expression of the principle of will. It is life-giving, vibrant, and vital. It dances and flickers about like the flame of a candle, full of radiant energy.

Joy is a very busy kind of energy, almost always associated with achievement. It expresses itself through activity, not through immobility, passiveness or rest. This activity of joy is a point which must be stressed, for many spiritually motivated people have formed entirely mistaken impressions of joy. They believe that joy is some sort of mystical stupor of ecstasy which more closely resembles catatonia than activity. In large part, this misunderstanding is the result of observing the Oriental gurus who have become so popular in this country today, and who are often received without intelligent examination. To the Easterner, joy is usually associated with being very "nice" in the conventional sense—extremely placid, always smiling, and quite harmless. Of course, there may be virtue in this state compared to what these people would be like otherwise, but it has nothing whatsoever to do with being joyful. Typically, the person who follows the Oriental regime becomes dull, listless, humorless, and incoherent. Joy is not dullness! It is the expression of creative achievement. Joy is not listlessness! It is a state of great activity. Joy is not humorlessness! The primary hallmark of joy is an excellent sense of humor that snaps, crackles, and pops with wit. Joy is not incoherent! It is a function of the mind and thrives only where there is clear perception and the capacity to discern reality.

Part of the problem lies in most people's lack of knowledge of the higher realms of human existence. A common misconception, for example, is that the nirvanic (atmic) state of bliss is a completely passive loss of identity in a vast ocean of consciousness. Nothing could be more removed from reality, however, for the inherent nature of the atmic plane is intelligent activity. Thus, bliss is the epitome of human involvement. And since joy is a reflection of bliss in the mind of mankind, then obviously intelligent achievement is the very heart of this "something extra."

Indeed, the most notable examples of joy confirm this basic principle. There is, for instance, the dramatic story of Archimedes, the Greek mathematician and inventor. Archimedes was asked by his friend Hieron II, king of Syracuse, to test the purity of a gold crown. Hieron had given gold to a smith for the purpose of making the crown, but began suspecting that the smith had cheapened the purity of the gold with silver. At first, Archimedes was at a loss as to how to conduct such a test. But the needed flash of insight came to him as he stepped into a tub filled with water at the public baths. He observed that the bulk of his body displaced some of the water in the bath, causing it to spill over. He then calculated that the amount of water displaced was equal to the bulk of his body;

furthermore, as silver is lighter than gold, a pound of silver will be bulkier than a pound of gold and will therefore displace a greater amount of water. The ingenuity of this simple test for the purity of gold delighted and thrilled Archimedes, and he jumped out of the bath shouting, "Eureka! Eureka!" In Greek, that expression means, "I have found it!" In his enthusiasm, he forgot to dress himself and ran naked through the streets of Syracuse with only one idea in mind: to go home and test his inspiration. This he did and found that Hieron's suspicions were well-founded: the crown was not pure gold. It can be imagined that this discovery did not cause the smith any measure of joy, but Archimedes' delight was obviously unalloyed. He had accomplished something of great moment and importance, and the thrill of creativity rushed through him like a mighty current. He was overwhelmed by the power of his insight, was lifted up to a wholly new level of vision and comprehension, and momentarily became oblivious to everything lesser.

An even more spectacular example of joy can be found in the book of Genesis. Here the mathematician and inventor is not Greek, but Universal: He is God. The richness of joy permeates the entire process of Creation, as told symbolically in this account. Consider, for example, the passage: "And God said, 'Let there be light,' and there was light. And God saw that the light was good." Hidden within these few words is a great revelation of the nature of joy, which can be seen by anyone with eyes to see. God saw that what He had made was good, and He rejoiced in His work; He delighted in His creation. And this joy spurred Him on to further creativity; the joy at the end of the first day led Him to pursue His work on the second day, which built momentum for the third day, and so on through the whole process. It is joy which characterizes the tempo of God's work, right up to the end of the sixth day, when He created man and woman in His own image and saw that His work was very good, and blessed His entire creation. Indeed, the mood of joy is so very much present in this divine act of creativity that one is almost tempted to believe that the godly image from which the pattern of man and woman was drawn was the *image of joy!*

Of course, few of us are inventors like Archimedes, and none of us is the Universal Mathematician. But while our own personal manifestations of joy may not be as memorable as these two examples, it is nonetheless important that we, too, can learn to express joy through our own achievements, big or small. And when we have tasted joy and learned what it is, we can then weave it into the fabric of our life and make it an integral part of our being. For joy is not some rare essence that can only be captured in peak moments in the bathtub or at the Creation of the world. Instead, it is an enduring, active force which can be known and expressed every moment of a person's life, bubbling up from the clear springs of humanity within. If we are to be artists of life, we cannot choose to turn our artistic ideals on and off depending on the vagaries of the moment. We must strive to express the highest degree of art every moment of every day. Thus, joy must become a constant presence for us, a constant though spontaneous dwelling in enthusiasm, delight, and vitality which can help us face the difficult and despairing moments of life as well as help us celebrate the moments of great breakthrough.

Joy heals, joy lifts up, joy harmonizes. It can be found wherever human life is found; it can be expressed in any circumstance, in any surroundings. It can be learned by the person who feels stuck in a dreary, uninspiring job in an office with drab walls, as well as by the person who has just the kind of job he or she prefers. It can be expressed by the housewife who has to diaper babies' bottoms and scrub floors, as well as by the person who leads a free and independent life. It can be known by the blue collar worker and the white collar worker equally; it is not the privilege of any segment or class of society. It can be known by the minister in his pulpit, by the teacher in his classroom, by the psychiatrist at his desk, and by his client on the couch. And when joy is expressed, it transfigures what once might have been dull and uninspiring; it gives new life, new purpose, and new fulfillment. The office worker who discovers joy begins to find new possibilities and new satisfaction in the same job he once considered a dead end; he feels less restricted and more in harmony with his mates and superiors. The housewife who trades in her complaints for joy begins to find new significances and rewards in the raising of children and the management of a household.

No, joy is not happiness; it is not just a mirthful response to what is happening to us. It is truly a "something extra" which lifts us out of the merry-go-round realm of illusion into clearer perception, into greater fulfillment. Nor is it an abstract imagining of poetic minds; it is real and has substance. It is a tool for active participation in daily life and can be cultivated by anyone interested in learning the art of living. And the reward for the effort is great and good, for the reward is a seat at the feast in the hall of reality, the feast of ambrosia and nectar.

Anyone who has tasted and sipped of the essence of joy knows that it is a sustaining force of rare degree. It is indeed food, but no ordinary food. It lifts up the heart of mankind and gives new purpose; it infuses the mind of man with new inspiration. It makes the mortal immortal.

Delightenment

Joy can perhaps be best defined as the delight in achievement and accomplishment. The accomplishment can be big or small; if it is genuine, it will bring joy. When a person is just beginning to learn to express joy, this delight in accomplishment will probably only occur as the result of his or her own achievements, and possibly the achievements of friends and colleagues. Later, as the individual develops a more universal consciousness and a greater awareness of joy, he will begin to express joy simply because humanity itself is growing, maturing, and accomplishing worthwhile goals. The awareness of the achievements of mankind becomes a constant realization for him, and thus even in moments that lack personal accomplishment, he can be filled with joy.

It is, however, important to have a true understanding of what achievement and accomplishment are. An individual can conceptualize a new idea, but that by itself is not an accomplishment. The idea must be produced—it must be made manifest and given shape, color, and function. And, it must be shared with others. Then and only then will it become an achievement which can be delighted in and rejoiced about.

Ultimately, as we grow in spiritual wisdom, we begin to see that the one great achievement of life is enlightenment. And so we set about perfecting the art of living, and as we do, our understanding of joy acquires new significance. We begin to discover that in this art, every day can bring fresh achievements of great value; thus, every day can bring new joy. Soon, and in very practical terms, joy does become a constant sharing in universal consciousness; it becomes a habitual mood with which we greet every moment.

In this fashion, we quickly grow into what should truly be called a state of *delightenment*—a wonderful state of delighting in our constantly increasing enlightenment and the constantly increasing enlightenment of all mankind and civilization. This is joy: a state of being lit up with life, of shining that light into the whole world, and of delighting in the recognition of the light in all forms of life everywhere. Delightenment is the gift of the Midas touch—not to turn everything we touch into gold, but to touch everything we can with the sparkling effervescence of joy.

It should be obvious, then, that joy is actually a mood of the inner being, of the soul. It is ever the soul that delights in achievement; it is ever the soul that perceives human growth and is pleased. Of course, a mood of the soul is something quite different than a mood of the personality. Moods of the personality, such as happiness, fluctuate and vary. They are caused by reactions to the moment. By contrast, moods of the soul are constant states of realization—unshakeable and real.

In other words, at our innermost levels of being, we are constantly expressing joy. Life may be hellish in the outer realms of the personality, but nonetheless the soul knows joy. The soul knows delightenment.

Why? Quite simply, because joy is a natural state of existence at the inner level of being, just as having a heart and a brain is a natural state of existence on the physical level. Joy is part of the basic equipment of the inner being, and this is true for an unadvanced person as well as for a highly developed being. Any entity (in this case, the soul) that can create such a complex mechanism as even a primitive human personality is obviously capable of expressing great joy. For joy is the natural product of perfectly understanding the nature of our identity and our relationship to other life in the universe. It is the product of perfectly understanding our purpose and work and of making the effort to fulfill that purpose. The soul has this basic self-realization and therefore knows joy.

Thus, our capacity to know joy and to express delightenment will depend to a large degree upon our understanding of the role we play in life (as a personality) and upon our contact and rapport with the inner being, our soul. It will also depend upon our level of enlightenment and upon the true comprehension of our self-identity. And, it will likewise depend upon our ability to delight in the wisdom and benevolence and smooth functioning of the world.

Joy grows as our understanding of ourself and of the universe in which we live grows. But there is another requirement as well. Joy grows as we achieve greater expression of the inner purpose of our being at the level of our personality. In other words, even though joy is a quality of the soul, it nonetheless constantly seeks to be grounded in the physical and the emotional realms of the personality. In partially enlightened people, the manifestation of joy will occur only from time to time. In fully enlightened people, it will be a constant expression. But no matter how little we have been expressing joy until now, we can resolve to strive for its full expression in our daily life.

An important point to inject here is that many people express joy without being aware of any conscious contact with their soul. After all, only a very small number of people have conscious awareness of being in contact with their soul. In comparison, the number of people who express joy at least occasionally is much greater. Actually, any expression of joy should be seen as evidence that some kind of direct contact does exist between the soul and the personality, and as evidence that the soul approves of and rejoices in at least some part of the effort the personality is making.

Thus, while joy is a mood of the soul, the only effective measuring stick for deciding how much joy we express is the personality. We must try to decide how much of the joy of the soul is seeping through the personality into expression—and what we can do to open up the personality for a greater expression of this something extra of delightenment.

It would be impractical to list here all of the possible ways of manifesting joy in physical expression. All events of life contain the seed for the expression of joy. It is perhaps most natural to express joy after making some great mental discovery, or in the process of traditional creativity—writing, painting, sculpting, acting, dancing, or whatever. But the richest possible expression of delightenment, of course, comes in perfecting the art of living. Can there be a better way of displaying joy, for example, than by delighting in the building of a right relationship with another human being—a vital relationship which will inspire both people to greater growth, maturity, and love? Or, can we imagine a more satisfying form of joy than the delight gained in finding meaning and purpose in some aspect of life that other, less inspired people find dull? It is a real achievement to be able to take a seemingly menial task—either at work or at home—and transform it into something that expresses our humanity and ingenuity. Such achievements inevitably trigger joy, by evoking a deeper interest in the way the world works and in the way that consciousness expresses itself.

Any effort at improving one's life is an excellent way of stimulating joy. The achievement of a certain amount of detachment, for example, is a cause for great rejoicing and will invoke the delight of the soul in the success of the personality. The successful elimination of a distressful habit pattern and its replacement by a better one is likewise a cause for celebration. The development of a new skill or talent—be it playing the piano, improving concentration, or developing a new degree of intuition—will similarly produce joy.

A growth in maturity, a deeper understanding of the purposes of mankind, a greater ability to think—all of these will prove torchbearers for joy. And so, even though we do not all have the opportunity to be an Archimedes or a Rembrandt, we all do have the opportunity—the option, to be more precise—to become master builders of right relationships, master craftsmen of inspired living, and master draftsmen of perfect habit patterns. In other words, we all have ample opportunity to make delightenment a reality in our lives—simply by expressing it. We do not have to wait for it to "magically" appear (so that we may be joyful). Waiting for joy is a fruitless process. We find joy by *putting it into our life*, by engaging in activities that draw a joyous response from the soul. We become joyful by *filling our life with joy*.

The Ways Joy Works

Happiness could be called "an end in itself," to use a common phrase. It culminates an effort. Joy, however, should be called "a beginning in itself," for it is much more than just pure delight. It is a living energy which marks the beginning of innovation and further growth. It does not merely celebrate a certain accomplishment, but also leads on to further evolution, further advancement, and further achievement. Joy releases a quality of life which permeates consciousness and works toward a transformation of understanding, skills, and talents. This quality of life, which is really a derivative of the will to live, produces a number of important effects within us which are worth examining in some detail. They can be catalogued as follows:

Joy is a motivator. It fills us with enthusiasm. Its presence causes us to delight in the work we are doing. In this way it builds momentum to give us the initial desire to begin a creative project (for example, in the art of living), and it keeps us on the job once we have begun to work. Without joy, we need some kind of artificial stimulus to get us to work and to keep us going—a stimulus such as money or fear.

Of course, joy is not motivation itself; it is a mood which releases motivation and indicates to us what the innermost motive for the art of living is. But that inner motivation cannot be tapped and known by a human being except through the development of joy.

It seems to be popular in this modern day to belittle the worth of work and proper motivation. The "work ethic" is abused; it is not *chic*. But then again, that may explain why being chic is so often a joyless state.

Joy is a healing force. It is the mood in which the soul created the personality, and it is likewise the mood in which the inner being goes about the work of healing the personality, when that is necessary. Again, it is not precisely joy that performs the healing work, but the entire healing process is greatly augmented by the presence of joy. This holds true for healing not only the physical body, but the emotional body and the mind as well—every aspect of the personality.

On the mental level, an inflow of joy tends to stimulate the mind and make it more alert. The apathetic mind, for example, will find a powerful antidote in the stuff of joy. Similarly, the mind which has been imprisoned by illusion will find that the process of cleaning out the debris of old thought-forms proceeds far more quickly when approached with joy.

On the emotional level, joy tends to heal depression and despair. The state of being downcast, grim, and excessively sober about life is actually a state of joylessness. If a person who is afflicted by depression would open himself up to the presence of joy, then much of the feeling of defeat and despair could be alleviated. The pattern of constantly wallowing in the depths of negativity would be broken up by the act of reaching up to higher levels of awareness.

Physically, the person who has learned to express joy will on the average be less vulnerable to illness and better equipped to overcome that which does come his way, for he has a more thorough understanding of the meaning and purpose of all aspects of his life. The person who can grasp the hidden purposes being worked out by an illness will be better able to overcome it quickly than the individual who sees sickness as just a meaningless (and threatening) event in his life.

On every level, the healing flow of joy cleanses the personality; it breaks up the logjam of piled up thoughts and conflicts in the subconscious. It relieves our mental indigestion and constipation. In this sense, the healing aspect of joy acts as a lubricant which oils the mechanism of consciousness. It keeps us from overheating, it smooths away the roughness of life, and it cuts down on the friction which is a part of everyday living. In general, it makes us more efficient.

Joy is a balancer. It is a sure indicator of proper perspectives; it is a compass which always lets us step back from the full flush of our activities and see all of the alternatives. It leads us out of the hall of the banquet of illusion into the hall of the feast of the real. It produces the balance and poise which give us this kind of detachment. And in the process, joy relieves stress of all kinds. Stress is merely the result of imbalance. With the return of balance, stress is eliminated.

One of the clearest examples of how joy can be used to restore balance in a person's life is the effectiveness of humor in relieving stress. Humor is one of the principal hallmarks of joy; the joyful person always has an abundance of wholesome, good humor, which aids him in keeping his life in balance. In difficult situations, the gift of humor helps him avoid being carried away with the emotions of the moment; it helps remind him of the larger principles upon which he bases his life. For instance, it often occurs that two people become embroiled in an intense argument over an issue that is quite silly. In the heat of their emotions, they lose sight of the essential silliness of the argument, and the conflict becomes bitter. However, if one of them can catch himself and realize that the difference is being carried to absurd extremes—and that the whole scene is quite foolish and laughable—he can avoid being sucked into the full emotionalism of the argument. He can step back sufficiently to be able to chuckle at the obvious absurdity of the situation, and may often be able to succeed in getting the other person to see the humorous aspects of their conflict as well.

Joy can provide just that kind of balance.

As our appreciation and expression of joy increases, so does our sense of humor and the ability to use it in this manner. Naturally, this use of joy is a most valuable tool in the art of living, and one which can be applied in many ways—not just to end a silly argument. The capacity to laugh at ourself and at the situations we must face is a great gift and a sure sign of maturity. It is frequently our rescue and our salvation.

If we find ourself suddenly filled with great fear, for example, but can step back enough to see the ludicrous nature of our fear (and all fears are ludicrous), it will then be possible to laugh gently at ourself and banish the fearfulness from our mind. Laughter is a mighty weapon; it literally destroys any negativity on contact. Similarly, if we find ourself depressed, we can take a moment to contemplate how utterly absurd it is ever to allow ourself to be depressed, even for a brief minute. There is so much beauty and joy and awe-inspiring glory in this universe of ours that it is absolutely comedic that we should be so silly. And so, having been guided back to our senses by recalling the presence of joy, we laugh at ourself gently and restore our equilibrium.

Of course, this matter of laughing at ourself requires a delicate and proper touch. It would be harmful to be cruelly sarcastic of ourself, for instance. Rather, we must learn that balanced ratio of good humor and intelligent insight which is so marvelously portrayed by the fairy sprite Puck in Shakespeare's *A Midsummer Night's Dream*. In this play Puck has the assignment of helping the various mortal lovers stay out of serious mischief and yet fall in love with the persons they are supposed to marry—not an easy task at all. The result is confusion, heated emotions, intrigue, and—eventually—success. Puck finds humor in it all, saying: "And those things do best please me/That befall preposterously." He also learns a thing or two about the human condition and sums it all up in his classic statement: "Lord, what fools these mortals be!"

Let this be our motto, then: "Lord, what fools we mortals be!" When we start to succumb to despair or fear, or strife of any kind, let us remember this phrase and repeat it as though it were a mantra. In this way, we can attune ourself once more to the constant presence of joy and let it flood our whole awareness. Thus, we restore balance. It is natural for men and women to be foolish every now and then, so there is really no cause for shame and despair—these are just absurd reactions. Rather, we must laugh a little at our grimness and excessive seriousness, shake our heads bemusedly and then get back to the task at hand. The joyful person can do this much more easily than the joyless one.

Joy is an integrating force. It harmonizes the diverse aspects of the personality, so that they cohere and function in unison. Such harmonization is of great significance, as it is the key to maturity and mental health. Without it, the personality would have no chance to become strong and dynamic. But joy does more than just integrate the different elements of the personality. It also integrates the harmonized personality with the soul, and it is this integration which eventually produces enlightenment. Joy stirs up within us our deepest intellectual and spiritual capacities and links them with our daily functioning vehicles for thought, feeling, and activity. Gradually, it attunes the outer vehicles with the inner capacities, until they become one and the same, united. Joy makes our emotions and thoughts and physical body receptive to inner inspiration and also causes us to continually "ground" this inner inspiration through the outer personality. In this way, it forces the integration of the soul and the personality.

Of course, this dramatic-sounding process actually works out in many ordinary ways. We may, for example, achieve a good measure of integration through something as commonplace as an absorbing hobby. The pursuit of the hobby causes us to seek the inspiration of the inner being—its guidance and creativity. And the time we spend engaged in the hobby gives the inner being the opportunity to ground itself through the mind, the emotions, and the physical body.

It is for this reason that hobbies frequently play an important role in our mental health and growth. For many people, their hobbies are the only aspects of their lives in which they permit joy to well up from within. Thus, the hobbies provide the sole opportunity for integrating the personality.

Naturally, the wise person will see that these principles of integration can and should be applied to every aspect of life. In other words, he will try to express joy as a constant presence.

Joy is a vitalizing force. The acts of rejoicing and enjoyment are not just releases of pent up feelings. They are actually bursts of new life and vitality. It is this new energy which fuels continued innovative efforts. Joy, therefore, is an important aspect of creativity.

In fact, the mood of joy is the mood of

creativity. After all, joy is a mood of the soul. And what does the soul do? It creates. It creates the physical body, the emotions, and the mind, and it sustains this threefold personality throughout life. It also creates the conditions that the personality must work with in its life—the opportunities, the handicaps, the good luck, and the obstacles. It does all this with the ultimate goal of being able to create a personality which is capable of demonstrating the joy, the love, the wisdom, and the light of the inner realms of existence.

The roots of all creativity are found within, in the region of the soul. Our acts of creativity are born deep within us, at this level of abstract being. Here the first flash of inspiration is conceived and begins to take shape as a practical expression. As an idea, it remains for awhile at this level, building up intensity. It is at this point that the vitalizing capacity of joy becomes important. The soul's mood of joy infuses the creative idea with certain potent life energies which give it the dynamic push to seek manifestation. In this sense, joy is very much like a flame that produces not only light but also heat. Not only does joy create a sense of delight at the potential of this new creative idea, but it also generates the energies which will transform the potential into manifestation.

Once the creative idea has gestated in this fashion, it then begins flowing downward into the personality with great power—assuming that we are open to creative inspiration and have removed all roadblocks in the subconscious which might otherwise interfere. The inspiration enters the mind and becomes known consciously to us as an idea. If the idea is welcomed, then over a period of time it becomes clothed with mental energy, taking shape more definitely in the mind's eye. But with this creative inspiration also comes the same mood of joy which infused the idea with life at the level of the soul. The joy protects and nourishes the creative idea as it is being translated in the mind, and helps condition the mind to work with the new idea. It tends to produce in us a sense of enthusiasm—the enthusiasm which will give us the motivation to initiate this creative project.

As this occurs, the idea is precipitated also into the astral body, causing an emotional reaction. We form either a like or a dislike for the idea; if the former, we then begin building up a strong desire to see it through to manifestation. The basic stimulus of this desire is, of course, the steady pressure of the joy of the inner being. Finally, even the sluggish physical mechanism is stirred into action, and the creative idea finds complete manifestation on the physical plane—as a novel, a painting, a new invention, an improved relationship, a fresh approach to raising children, a new understanding of other people, an additional use of intuition, or whatever it may be.

In this way, the inner being uses the quality of joy and the process of creativity to add new life to the personality, to introduce new vitality and inspiration into its daily affairs. Creativity is not just a process of rearranging existing variables—it is innovation, the production of something better. Working creatively with the emotions, for example, is not just a question of rearranging emotional hang-ups and problems so we can live with them more easily. Emotional perfection is not achieved by repressing our worries and fears through hypnosis, nor by releasing our hates and frustrations through screaming and pounding and wailing. Nor is it just a bland state of emotional calmness which really amounts to being an emotional eunuch. True creativity goes much deeper. It is analogous to the work of the village smithy, standing at his forge, melting ingots of iron and then hammering that red-hot iron into entirely new forms of practical use. We must take the raw material of our emotions and traits, melt it in the forge of our creativity with the heat of our joy, and then hammer the red-hot essence into wholly new expressions of love, affection, tenderness, and kindness which are appropriate for our relationships, our needs, and our life. We must then express these pure emotional forms in our life, striving as we do to express also the joy with which we created them. We must use them as powerful tools for communicating with others, for helping others to see more clearly, and for touching others with hope, compassion, and inspiration.

Nor does the creative use of the mind have anything to do with being a better sophist than others or being able to manipulate the thoughts of others. Rather, it involves being able to illuminate our thoughts with a much higher quality of life, and being able to mold mental energy into precise forms which can serve as vehicles for the constructive use of the mind: for healing, teaching, and inspiring.

At the end of the creative process, the vitalizing quality of joy most naturally expresses itself as a celebration of the achievement, and this then prepares the way for further creativity. No constructive, affirmative act in this universe is ever wasted or forgotten; every achievement we make in our life opens the door for a greater inflow of the vitality of life into our own consciousness. It is this new inflow of life, indeed, which gives us great delight and makes us want to shout with Archimedes, "Eureka! Eureka!" It makes us want to rejoice, to shout from the top of the mountain that we have reached a new peak. This urge to celebrate should not be repressed: it should be given vent. For it signifies the birth of a new measure of life—a measure of life which will have a profound impact upon what we are able to achieve in the future.

Becoming Joyful

Any effort to increase our understanding and expression of joy must begin where joy exists—on the mental plane. In other words, we must begin by *thinking*. And, as much as possible, we must try to think as the soul thinks, for joy is a fundamental mood of the inner being.

But what should we think about?

In the first place, we should think about those aspects of our life which are causes for rejoicing. In all likelihood, we will have to start by throwing out and revising a large number of basic assumptions about our life in order to do this, because many of us—

having never thought about joy before—would immediately conclude that there is little if anything *worth* rejoicing in. We are still stuck in the banquet of illusion. But in point of fact, each one of us can find many, many aspects of life worthy of our delight.

Then we can add to that the contemplation of how the inner being views and regards our life. What is the inner being's purpose? What is it trying to accomplish? How is it seeking to express greater joy? Again, we will have to be prepared to revise many of our thoughts and attitudes if this particular line of thought is to succeed. After all, very few of us are used to thinking—we have just been reacting emotionally all of our life. That will not suffice if we are seeking to become joyful. We must start using our minds. We must escape the bewilderment of illusion.

To this activity we can eventually add another: the contemplation of the purpose and role of mankind, and the realization that our participation in the activities of mankind enriches our own life and gives us joy. To be effective, we will have to broaden our perspectives and overcome our selfish limitations. We will have to give up our prejudices and our stereotyped notions. All of these thought-forms will have to be cleared away, so we can indeed begin thinking. Then we can start considering how much mankind as a whole is growing, and in this way we can begin delighting in these accomplishments as well as our own. In doing this, it is important not to get sidetracked and bogged down in the mass consciousness of fears, hatreds, and worries that afflict the average person in the world today. Again, these are illusions and emotional reactions. Rather, we must see the advancements in human caring, in international rapport, in science, in education, and in the many, many other fields in which there have been significant achievements in the last few hundred years.

Obviously, the success of this thinking will depend to a large degree upon our ability to think about these issues with detachment—with the poise of the soul. The mastery of the practice of detachment is a necessary first step to becoming joyful.

But abstract thinking by itself, while a good beginning, is not enough. It merely prepares the mind to handle joy. We must also seek to be more innovative in our life, knowing that it is through the activity of achievement that joy finds expression. Of course, this does not mean that we must rush out and join a painting class or start writing poetry. Creative expression can indeed be found in such traditional forms of art, but we must always remember that the most important area of creativity is the art of living. This is an art that uses our moods, emotions, thoughts, habits, relationships, and spoken words as the raw materials for creating masterpieces of beauty. It is an art that finds inspiration in the circumstances of our life as they exist now—the conditions of our work, the nature of our home life, the inner content of the subconscious, and so on. Perhaps these conditions do not seem very artistic at present, but that is precisely why they are such apt vehicles for increasing our creativity and thus our joy. They can be *made* artistic.

By deliberately trying to make the variables of our life creative, we can succeed in becoming joyful. There really is no other way. If we have an unpleasant job, we do not become joyful by quitting the job and trying to find one that suits us better. There is no joy in running away from situations we cannot handle or in avoiding people we dislike. Joy always comes through achievement—by taking a difficult job and making it satisfying, by discovering a creative way of improving our relationship with someone we have not liked, or by putting joy into aspects of life we once thought joyless. And joy only comes through individual self-initiative. It is not given to us by angels blowing golden trumpets—it is released by our own efforts. We must blow the trumpets ourself!

Most importantly, however, we must seek to enjoy life in all its aspects—even the trials, the struggles, and the crises. We must try to make delightenment a general attitude with which we meet every event and every moment of our life.

There is more than one way to walk down a road. We can walk straight and uprightly, sure of our footing, with dignity, grace, and joy. Or, we can stumble clumsily along, like a drunk. Even worse, if we break a leg, we have to limp along, propped up by crutches. Just so, there is more than one way to tread the path of personal growth and enlightenment. We can approach our growth with eagerness and joy, delighting in every step of the way and never letting obstacles or adversity either slow the pace or dim our joyfulness. Or, we can become very serious and stamp out every trace of humor and levity. We can plod along with heavy foot, talking grimly of the terrible struggle we are undergoing, about the "dark night of the soul" we are facing, about the crosses we must bear, and so on. We can become obsessed with suffering and in the process suffer immensely.

Or, worse yet, we can put on a very sour countenance, whining and moaning about every step we take. We can complain about all the evil around us—especially the evil in others; we can jabber foolishly about original sin and fire and brimstone. We can, in short, succeed in making our pathway a living hell.

The road of whining and moaning is a grossly unintelligent way to tread the path; it is a regression, not a progression—a dehumanizing curse upon mankind. But in truth the road of the self-styled martyr and sufferer is not very much better. It, too, is an unintelligent approach which impedes growth more than it encourages it. And yet there are many good people who have devoted themselves to the eventual goal of enlightenment who have not learned the dangers of this path. They consider it a spiritual virtue to deny themselves, to be contrite to the point of groveling, and to be perfectly miserable most of the time. They have not learned the virtue of expressing joy.

We do not tread the pathway for ourself alone. Our progress makes it easier for those who will follow us at a later time—and there are billions yet to come—to find the path and make their progress. If we litter the pathway to enlightenment with the beer cans of our suffering, with the plastic wrappers of our depression, with the garbage of our adversity, and the broken glass of our excessive seriousness, we will be doing those who follow a great disservice. Not only will they have to make their own effort, but they will also have to pick up our litter! Nor is this description just a clever metaphor. There is a pathway, and it does collect and permanently record our attitudes and moods. We leave indelible marks along the way.

To put it quite plainly, an emphasis upon struggle, hardship, and suffering is incompatible with true growth and spiritual realization. As Saint Francis de Sales said it, "A saint who is sad is a sad saint." Groveling has no place in the thinking of a person sincerely interested in perfecting the art of living.

It may be objected by some that such an attitude is unrealistic, that there is suffering along the way; there are obstacles to be overcome and adversity to be faced. There are temptations and trials. The dark night is an undeniable experience which all must face.

True. But each of us has the option as to how we will face these obstacles. It is possible to see an obstacle ahead and weep with despair. But it is also possible to see the same obstacle and react with great joy, knowing that the obstacle presents a challenge which will help us develop talents and strengths which can then aid us in treading the pathway more rapidly. Obviously, this is the healthier response.

Thus, it is important to cultivate a joyful outlook as we proceed along the way. Not only will it make our efforts easier, but it will also greatly help those who are yet to come. For, rather than leaving behind us litter which might cause some of them to stumble and fall, we are leaving behind us little lights that will help them see more clearly where the path begins and where it leads. We are leaving behind guideposts and helpful assistance. And that in itself is a form of unselfish, constructive achievement.

Therefore, let us not begrudge what we must do. Instead, let us wade into it with enthusiasm, delighting in our opportunities to contribute to the growth of mankind. We must not sulk in the face of adversity, but instead rest cheerfully in the assurance that "my yoke is easy, and my burden is light." We must stand confident in our joy and let others see it. It is far healthier to skip and dance our way merrily along the path—even if we may be accused by some of being irreverent—than to plod along solemnly as though the full weight of the world were on our shoulders.

Truly, Isaiah knew whereof he spoke when he said: "With joy you will draw water from the wells of salvation." There is no other way.

Worthy of Immortality

The rewards of joy are many. One of the greatest is that joy helps lead us out of the hall of illusion into the hall of reality. Joy helps us put our life into better perspective; we begin to see more clearly the gains we have made, the opportunities which have opened up for us, the good people we are friends with and the good times we have shared with them, and the capacity we have built up for expressing our inner humanity. We begin to think.

Then, too, joy is a signal of the satisfaction of the inner being. Happiness comes with the fulfillment of the desires of the personality. Joy, on the other hand, comes with the fulfillment of the will of the soul. Thus, the surging up of joy from within is a sure indication that the soul is pleased with what the personality has accomplished, just as God was pleased at the end of each day of Creation when He gazed at all that He had wrought and sighed: "It is good." Can the personality ever hope for any greater reward than a sign that its inner being is pleased?

Moreover, as we develop our joyfulness, we enlarge our capacity to share in universal consciousness. We begin to understand that when we are joyful we are in a very real sense giving voice to God's delight in the world. We embody the abstract and give it form, so that others may see it, too. In truth, joy is not personal at all; it is universal. It is God's joy, not ours alone.

This universal awareness can greatly enrich our life. The light in which we delight lets us see the light which surrounds us on all sides—the light in other people, the light in other dimensions, the light in all of life. We spontaneously begin to see the nobility and perfection inherent in all life, in ourself, and in God's design for us. We become conscious of the growing presence of universal awareness in our hearts and in our minds. We develop the eyes to see, the ears to hear, the mind to know, and the heart to feel.

On the personality level, the joyful person is rewarded in many ways. He begins to extend the scope of his joyfulness in all directions. Whereas once he knew joy only under certain conditions and at certain times, he begins to express joy more constantly. He comes to find joy in the smallest of things—even the least important occurrences of life. It is not just when he discovers a great mathematical principle or achieves a major goal of life; it is also when he meets other people, when he goes to work in the morning, when he travels, when he relaxes—in short, in the ordinary course of daily life. He finds joy in commonplace circumstances not because they give him joy, but because he puts joy into everything he does. The joy is *within him,* and thus all of the circumstances of his life reflect that joy.

As a person becomes more joyful, his sense of humor deepens and becomes more ever-present, keener, and more refreshing. With it also comes greater flexibility and resilience; he is less rigid than before. He can bend rather than break—he is more tolerant and understanding, better able to withstand difficulties. Joy gives him a protection for the work which must be done, a shield against all the dangers that must be faced. The art of living does require facing our weaknesses and overcoming them, making the imperfect perfect. Without joy, we might well be overpowered by our weaknesses and imperfections. But with joy, we have the capacity and support to succeed.

And last but not least, joy is the "something extra" which lets us partake of the feast that has been prepared for us—the banquet of ambrosia and nectar. In Greek mythology, ambrosia and nectar are the divine food and drink upon which the gods sup. By becoming joyful, we can share in this abundance, too, and it can sustain us. But it can do even more. According to mythology, ambrosia and nectar have a hidden power: the power to keep a corpse from decay. In other words, they bestow immortality.

Joy bestows immortality upon us. Not immortality of the physical body, of course, for that will invariably die. Who would want to keep his physical body for all eternity anyway? Rather, joy lets us create manifestations of life that are *worthy* of immortality.

Worthy of immortality! How much of our lives are worthy of immortality? Immortality is not a gift bestowed on us on some mythical judgment day in the sky. It is an accomplishment which is earned through diligent effort. We achieve immortality by creating works that are worthy of lasting forever—for all eternity. These works are not physical works, of course. Rather, they are masterworks of human consciousness and talent: works of love, kindness, gentleness, affection, beauty, hope, faith, perception, aspiration, courage, strength, understanding, and many other humanistic qualities. These are the raw materials from which the important works of mankind are created. And when we have created a perfect expression of any of these qualities and skills, it then becomes a permanent part of our consciousness—and an inspiration for those who follow.

It is not the physical work of great people, after all, that lingers on (although it may be preserved for awhile); it is the quality of their consciousness. It is not the actual physical labor of Albert Schweitzer in his hospital in Africa, for example, which still exists. It is the quality of his love, his compassion, his dedication, and his intelligence. And those qualities are immortal—they will continue to inspire humanity long after the hospital is gone from the face of the earth.

This is, of course, the supreme creative effort—the effort to make something that will endure for all time. We build the best we can. Many times the results are quite remarkable. They endure for hundreds of years before we realize that we can do even better. And so we tear down and start all over again, from scratch, but with a better understanding of how to proceed. Thus, the next effort comes a good deal closer to being worthy of immortality. In this way, the process continues.

It is the nature of creation that only the good things—the very best of the best—will achieve immortality. All the rest—the cheap, the counterfeit, the seedy, the evil—will be torn down and destroyed sooner or later, to make way for better efforts. At the same time, however, it is also the nature of creation to encourage us to realize our role in this process and participate in it—as did Schweitzer and many, many others.

That is the true meaning of joy. It encourages us to participate in the effort of creation—to become worthy of immortality. It encourages us to partake of the feast in the banquet hall of the universe—to join in the divine celebration of life.

About the Authors

In the late 1960's, Dr. Robert R. Leichtman's interest in spiritual growth caused him to close his medical practice and devote his energies to lecturing, teaching, and writing. Dr. Leichtman is the developer of "Active Meditation," a comprehensive course in personal growth and meditative techniques. This teaching is aimed at helping people better understand their lives and develop intuitive skills. He is also the author of the paperback series, *From Heaven to Earth,* as well as *The Psychc Life, Psychic Vandalism, Psychic Self-Destruction, Fear No Evil, Faith Fatigue, The Curse of Fundamentalism, Recovering from Death and Other Disasters,* and the six-book subscription series, *Resurrecting Christianity*. Dr. Leichtman resides in Baltimore, where part of his time is spent continuing the healing work of Olga Worrall at the New Life Clinic.

Carl Japikse grew up in Ohio. A graduate of Dartmouth College, he began his work career as a newspaper reporter and freelance writer. He has worked for several newspapers, including *The Wall Street Journal*. In the early 1970's, he left the field of journalism and began pursuing his current interests: teaching personal and creative growth, lecturing, and consulting with businesses and individuals. Mr. Japikse is developer of "The Enlightened Management Seminar" and "The Enlightened Classroom," as well as various courses in spiritual growth, and the author of *The Light Within Us, Exploring the Tarot, The Hour Glass, The Primer of Love, Love Virtue, The Fabled Gate,*

Isms & Schisms, Light & Night, Fate, The Rising Mind, and, as Waldo Japussy, *The Tao of Meow, The Ruby Cat,* and *The Ethickal Cat.*

Together, Leichtman and Japikse are also authors of *The Life of Spirit* essay series, *Active Meditation: The Western Tradition, Forces of the Zodiac,* a seven-book set called *Enlightenment, Brainwashed!* and a four-book set of the I Ching: *Healing Lines, Ruling Lines, Connecting Lines,* and *Changing Lines.*

Ordering Additional Essays

Other essays issued in Enthea Press gift editions—the "Spiritual Companions" series—include *Working With Angels, Making Prayer Work, The Act of Meditation, Healing Emotional Wounds, Defeating Evil and Sin, The Role Death Plays in Life, The Noble Mind & Its Uses* and *The Way To Health*. They may be ordered by emailing Enthea Press at lig201@lightariel.com or by sending a check plus shipping to Enthea Press, P.O. Box 251, Marble Hill, GA 3018. Internet orders may be paid with PayPal. Visit our website at www.lightariel.com.

The other essays are available only in their original form—as one of six essays in each volume of *The Art of Living* and *The Life of Spirit*. These books can be ordered for $20 apiece, plus $6 for shipping, $8 if ordering two or more books. The entire set of either *The Art of Living* or *The Life of Spirit* can be bought for $90 each, postpaid, or both series can be ordered together for $160.

The Art of Living is also available in ebook format for $65.